A Magic Mouse Guide

E-mail

by
Chris Ward-Johnson
and the Magic Mouse

Illustrations & layout by
Laughing Gravy Design

Enslow Publishers, Inc.

40 Industrial Road	PO Box 38
Box 398	Aldershot
Berkeley Heights, NJ 07922	Hants GU12 6BP
USA	UK

http://www.enslow.com

Editor's note

Computers and e-mail software vary considerably. In this book we present information that is generally true of all PCs and e-mail systems and show a variety of particular screens. Do not worry if your screen is not the same as the one that appears in the book.

Acknowledgments

The publishers would like to thank the following for permission to use their photographs and copyright material:
Eudora; Netscape UK Ltd.

In memory of Jonathan Inglis

Library of Congress Cataloging-in-Publication Data

Ward-Johnson, Chris.
    E-mail : a magic mouse guide / Chris Ward-Johnson;
illustrations & layout by Laughing Gravy Design.
        v. cm. — (Magic mouse guides)
    Includes index.
    Contents: What is e-mail? — On the Internet — E-mail addresses —The right address — Make it snappy! — Say it with a smile — Sending your e-mail — Looking for a message — Receiving a message — Attachments — Sending a reply — Surprise, surprise! — More about e-mail.
    ISBN 0-7660-2261-7 (hardcover)
    1. Electronic mail systems—Juvenile literature. [1. E-mail. 2. Electronic mail systems.] I. Laughing Gravy Design. II. Title. III. Series: Ward-Johnson, Chris. Magic mouse guides.
    TK5105.73 .W37 2003
    004.692—dc21

                     2002013287

Printed in Dubai by Oriental Press.

10 9 8 7 6 5 4 3 2 1

To Our Readers:
We have done our best to make sure all Internet addresses in this book were active and appropriate when we went to press. However, the author and the publisher have no control over and assume no liability for the material available on those Internet sites or on other Web sites they may link to. Any comments or suggestions can be sent by e-mail to comments@enslow.com or to the address on the back cover.

First published by Cherrytree Books
(a member of the Evans Publishing Group)
327 High Street, Slough, Berkshire SL1 1TX, UK
Copyright © Evans Brothers Limited 2001
This edition published under licence from Evans Brothers Limited
All rights reserved
Designed and produced by A S Publishing
Illustrations and layout by Gary Dillon & Phil Jolly at Laughing Gravy Design

Contents

Mouse tips

Don't worry if your screen does not always look exactly like the ones in the book.

If there are words you don't understand, look on pages 28-31.

Mouse tips

What is e-mail?

Ben wants to ask Hari to come and play on Tuesday.

If he sends a letter now, it will not get to Hari's house until Wednesday.

Ben asks if he can phone Hari.

Hari is not there.
The phone rings
and rings. There is no
answering machine.

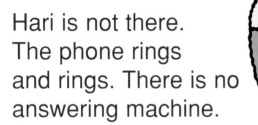

"Why don't you send an e-mail?" says
the Magic Mouse.

Sending an e-mail is like sending a
letter by telephone.

The "e" in e-mail stands
for electronic.

On the internet

"You can use my computer," says Ben's sister Liza.

To send an e-mail, you need a computer, a modem and an e-mail software program.

A modem links your computer to the internet. The internet is like a system of roads in a town. You can go from one address to another on the internet.

The internet is bigger than a town. It links addresses all over the world.

E-mail addresses

Everyone on the internet has an e-mail address. A pretend e-mail address might look like this:

suzymouse@mouseville.com

Your address starts with a name, followed by @. The @ sign means "at."

The next part of the address is the name of the company that links your computer to the internet.

An address that contains "edu" means it is a school or college.

Companies that link people to the internet are called internet service providers, or ISPs.

The letters "com" stand for company.

Ben's sister finds Hari's e-mail address.

Never give your e-mail address or real address to anyone you don't know.

The right address

Ben opens the e-mail program on Liza's computer. The screen looks like this:

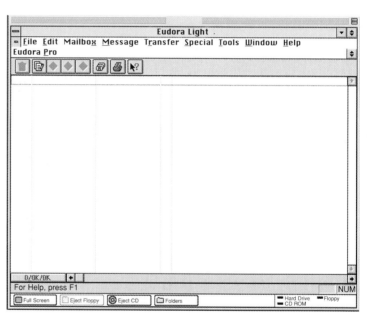

Ben clicks on Message and chooses New Message from the menu.

At the top of the window he types in Hari's address and checks it. He makes sure that he has got every letter, word and symbol just right. He remembers to use small letters and not to leave any spaces.

If one dot is out of place in the address, your e-mail will bounce. It will come straight back to your mailbox.

Copy the address exactly.
Don't leave spaces.

Make it snappy!

Now Ben writes a subject:
Come and play.
Underneath he types
his message.

Dear Hari,
It is my sister's birthday tomorrow.
She is going out with all her
friends in the afternoon. If you
come and play, we will have the
house to ourselves. Liza says we
can play on her computer.
Please reply, so that I can tell Mom.

See you
Ben.

SHOUT

Ben makes his message as short as possible. Short messages go quicker. He uses mostly small letters because BIG LETTERS on the internet are rude. Using them is like SHOUTING.

Some people use acronyms in their e-mails. These are a few letters that stand for a longer phrase. They may also use smileys. These are little pictures that tell the other person what you are feeling.

Time online can cost money. Always ask permission before you send an e-mail.

Say it with a smile

big grin

These are some acronyms that people use. You can make up your own. You can even have secret acronyms that only you and your friends know.

BTW	by the way
CU	see you
DL	download
FYI	for your information
IMO	in my opinion
LOL	laughing out loud
MYOB	mind your own business
OTT	over the top
ROFL	rolling on floor laughing
TIA	thanks in advance
TTFN	ta-ta for now
TY	thank you

wink

not a word

You make smileys using punctuation marks and keyboard characters. Look at them sideways and you see a face. Here are some smileys. See if you can make up some for yourself.

:-D	big grin	0:-)	angel
:'-(	boo hoo	:-P	tongue out
:-(	sad	:-{#}	smile with braces
:-)	happy		
;-)	wink	:-O	wow
:-x	not a word	$-)	greedy
:-/	what?	:*)	only joking

Smileys are also called emoticons.

sad

Only use an acronym if you know it will be understood. Otherwise you will waste time, not save it.

Sending your e-mail

Ben is ready to send his message. He checks the address and subject and clicks on Send. The computer dials up the service provider and the message whizzes off to Hari.

If the computer cannot get online immediately, it saves the message and tries again later. A message on the screen tells you whether your message has been sent or is waiting to go.

If you like, you can send the same message to more than one person at the same time.

It's a good idea to proofread your message before you click on the Send button.

Send

Sent

CC

Under the address box you will see another box saying "cc." In it you write the addresses of all the other people you want the same message to go to. The computer will send the message to all of them at once.

You can also send lots of different messages at one time.

Ben finds the e-mail addresses of some more of his and Liza's friends. He sends them all a message.

Subject: Surprise for Liza

Looking for a message

Ben hopes Hari is at home. He wants a reply.
Liza shows him how to check the mailbox and
tells him the password.

To find out if you have a message, you have to
go online and use a password. Ben opens the
e-mail window on his computer and clicks on
the item that searches for new mail.
He keys in the password.

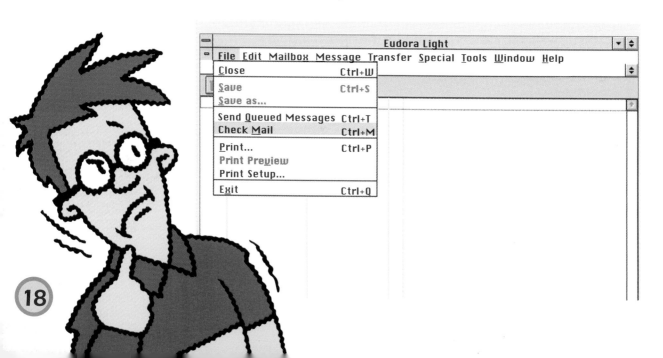

You have no new mail.

OK

After a while a message comes on the screen. It says that there's no new mail. Ben disconnects from the service provider and waits.

He tries again and again and there is still no reply.

You can e-mail anyone with an e-mail address— your favorite pop star or even Santa Claus.
Don't be disappointed if they are too busy to reply.

Receiving a message

At last! Ben tries once more before bedtime. This time the computer says that there is a message.

You have new mail.

OK

Ben watches as the message arrives.
It comes in to his mailbox and tells him
the sender, subject and date. He clicks
on the box and the full message
appears on the screen.

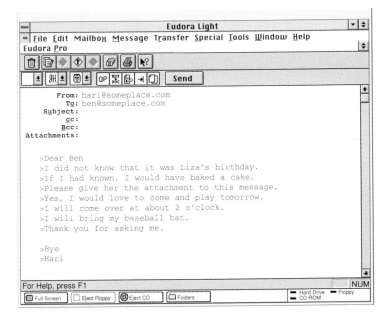

Attachments

Ben is pleased to get Hari's message.
He looks for the attachment. It is a file named
"Liza's card." He double-clicks on the file and
up comes a picture on the screen. Ben prints
out the file and keeps it for the next day.

You can print
out any e-mail
message and
some attachments.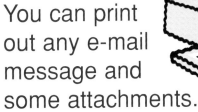
You do it in the same way that you
print any document.

You can send all kinds of things as
attachments.

- Any file on your computer.

- A drawing or a birthday card like
  Hari's.

- Sounds and videos.

- Pictures copied with a scanner.

- Photos taken with a digital
  camera.

Some e-mail programs
let you drag the attachment
on to your message.
Some use a menu or dialog
box to attach the file.

sending a reply

Next morning Ben checks the mailbox again. There are lots of messages and lots of attachments. They are all birthday messages and cards for Liza.

Liza reads them all and replies to them. It is easy to reply to e-mail messages.

You open the message you want to reply to. Then you click on the Reply item on the menu.

Reply

Reply

You can delete the original message if you want to or leave it.

Write your reply in its place or above it. Then click on Send and off it goes.

Liza sends one message to all her friends.

Surprise, Surprise!

It is 2 o'clock. Liza's friends come to take her out. But she is not going out. She is having a party.

Ben has sent e-mail invitations to all her friends and all his friends.

"Here they come!" says the Magic Mouse.
"Here they come!" says Mom.

Happy Birthday, Liza!

Always ask before
you invite anyone to
your house.
Never arrange to meet
anyone you don't know.

27

More about e-mail

@ Stands for the word "at."

Acronyms Initials used in place of whole words to save time.

Address Everyone on the internet has an address. The first part of an e-mail address is the user name, the second part is the symbol @, the third part is the domain, which tells you where the computer is. Only give your e-mail address to people you already know.

Address book Your software program lets you keep a file of names and e-mail addresses. You can type them in or copy them from e-mails you receive. Then when you want to send an e-mail all you need to do is click on the name and the message window will be prepared.

Attachment Any file from your computer that you attach to an e-mail. It can be text or a picture or an animated cartoon or sounds or videos or photographs. Keep attachments small to save time uploading and downloading.

Bouncing mail If you get an address wrong or if an address has changed, your message will bounce back to your mailbox.

cc To send a message to more than one person, fill in the other addresses in the box on your message heading and everyone you name will receive the e-mail.

Clicking Pressing and quickly releasing the mouse button. To double-click, quickly press and release the button twice. You will soon get to know when you need to click once or twice.

com Short for company.

Dialog box Window that lets you choose what you want to do next.

Digital camera A camera linked direct to your computer. You can take a picture, plug the camera into the computer and see the picture on-screen immediately or send it as an attachment.

Domain Part of an address that says what type of organization the computer is in (and sometimes where it is).

Download When a message or other

item is copied from the internet or from another computer to your computer, it downloads.

E-mail Electronic mail.

Emoticon Another name for smiley. It is made up of two words: emotion and icon.

File A single document or computer program.

Folder Place where you keep a group of files.

Flaming If you use CAPITALS or are rude, you may receive angry messages called flame mail.

Header The top part of an e-mail message that tells you about the sender, subject and receiver.

Icon A picture on your computer that you can open by double-clicking.

Internet A worldwide network of millions of linked computers.

Internet service provider A company that you pay to provide a link to the internet.

ISP Short for internet service provider.

Junk mail Advertisements and other unwanted mail that arrives unexpectedly. It is best to throw it away. Also called spam.

Mailbox The place where your computer stores incoming and outgoing e-mail messages.

Mailing lists Lists of people who share an interest and send each other articles. There are hundreds of topics to choose from. If you join a mailing list, you can talk to lots of people. You will also receive lots of mail that you may not want. So be careful before you put your address on a mailing list.

Menu A list of items for you to select from.

Modem An electronic device that sends computer signals through a telephone line.

Netiquette Good manners on the internet, including being brief and being polite.

Online When you are linked to the internet, you are online. When you are not linked, you are offline.

Password A set of characters and/or numbers that you key in to the computer to tell the service provider that it is you who wants to read your messages.

Program Set of electronic instructions that tells your computer what to do.

Punctuation marks Periods, commas, colons, question marks, quotation marks, like these — **. , : ? "** — that help make what you write easy to read.

Queue (Pronounced "Q") When your service provider cannot get online immediately your message stays in a queue.

Re:Mail See Reply.

Reply A quick way to send a reply to an e-mail. The To and Subject boxes are filled in for you. All you have to do is write your message and press Send.

Safety There are strange people on the internet. Some adults pretend to be children, so be careful.

- Never tell anyone where you live or where you go to school.

- Never give anyone your phone number.

- Never give anyone your password.

- Never arrange to meet anyone you do not already know.

- Never meet anyone without asking your parents first.

Scanner An electronic device that copies text or pictures onto your computer.

Send The icon or menu item you select to send your message.

Service provider Short for internet service provider.

Shouting Using CAPITAL LETTERS instead of small letters.

Signature A special way to sign your e-mails that you can create with some e-mail programs. You can use keyboard characters to draw your face.

Smiley A picture made from keyboard characters that tells the reader what you are feeling. Also called an emoticon.

Software Computer programs that you can use for various purposes. You need one to send e-mails.

Sounds You can record or download music and other sounds on to your computer and, if you have the right programs and equipment, attach them to e-mails.

Spam Another name for junk mail.

Videos If you have the right equipment and programs, you can send videos as attachments to your e-mails.

World wide web Collection of pages, or sites, on the internet that anyone with the right equipment can see.

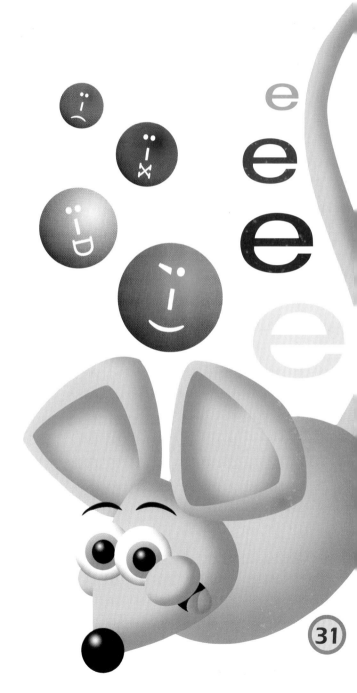

Index